SALMON

ELAINE ELLIOT AND VIRGINIA LEE

Photographed on location by Steven Isleifson

FORMAC PUBLISHING COMPANY LIMITED
HALIFAX 1996

PHOTO CREDITS:
All photographs by Steven Isleifson except where noted below:
Keith Vaughan — page 3 (top), 4

PARTICIPATING RESTAURANTS:

Acton's Grill and Café, Wolfville, NS
Bellhill Tea House, Canning, NS
Blomidon Inn, Wolfville, NS
Bluenose Lodge, Lunenburg, NS
Compass Rose Inn, Lunenburg, NS
Dalvay-by-the-Sea, Dalvay, PEI
Da Maurizio Dining Room, Halifax, NS
Drury Lane Steak House, Aulac, NB
Dufferin Inn and San Martello
   Diningroom, Saint John, NB
Dunes Café and Gardens, Brackley
   Beach, PEI
Haddon Hall, Chester, NS
Halliburton House Inn, Halifax, NS
Inn at Bay Fortune, Bay Fortune, PEI
Inn on the Cove, Saint John, NB

Inn on the Lake, Waverley, NS
La Perla Restaurant, Dartmouth, NS
Markland Coastal Resort, Dingwall, NS
Marshlands Inn, Sackville, NB
Murray Manor Bed and Breakfast,
   Yarmouth, NS
Nemo's Restaurant, Halifax, NS
Normaway Inn, Margaree Valley, NS
Pines Resort Hotel, Digby, NS
Quaco Inn, St. Martins, NB
Scanway Restaurant, Halifax, NS
Shaw's Hotel, Brackley Beach, PEI
Tea and Temptations English Tea Room,
   Dartmouth, NS

Dedication:

This book is dedicated to the memory of our parents, Margaret and Frank Stuart, who instilled in us a love of the Maritime way of life and taught us to believe in ourselves.

Canadian Cataloguing in Publication Data
Elliot, Elaine, 1939-
      Salmon
      (Maritime flavours series)
      ISBN 0-88780-352-0
1. Cookery (Salmon). 2. Cookery, Canadian -- Maritime Provinces.
I. Lee, Virginia, 1947- . II. Title. III. Series.
TX748.S24E44 1996   641.6'92   C95-950016-5

Formac Publishing Company Limited
5502 Atlantic Street
Halifax, N.S.
B3H 1G4

CONTENTS

INTRODUCTION *4*

APPETIZERS *7*

MAIN COURSES *25*

INDEX *64*

INTRODUCTION

*T*he very warm reception accorded our book, *Maritime Flavours Guidebook and Cookbook*, demonstrated that interest in the cuisine of the Maritime region is flourishing. The book also showed how you can prepare at home innovative recipes that professional chefs have developed in all three provinces.

In our visits to inns and restaurants over the years, one thing that has impressed us is the wide range of ideas that our best chefs have for including regional specialities. For this reason we decided to develop a series of four books that would celebrate the wonderful bounty of land and sea, in particular apples, blueberries, salmon, and lobster and other shellfish. We visited many of the inns and restaurants featured in *Maritime Flavours* and once again, the generosity of the chefs gave us an abundant selection of recipes with which to work. We selected the ones that would give the home cook a wide range of choice for enjoying the flavours of the region.

To round out each book, we added some tried and true recipes from our personal collections. All recipes have been tested in our homes and the quantities adjusted to serve four to six adults. For some recipes we have suggested low-fat alternatives.

Fine food presentation is an art, and one which is receiving increased emphasis by our chefs. What better way to describe how these recipes are presented by their originators than to show you! Photographer Stephen Isleifson visited our featured restaurants and photographed the dishes found in this *Maritime Flavours* series. What you see in these pages are the dishes as they are presented by their chefs, photographed on location.

Salmon has been a favourite at festive occasions for a long time. It has been one of the region's most celebrated specialities. There are classics, such as Poached Atlantic Salmon from Shaw's Hotel, Brackley Beach, PEI, in addition there are innovations such as Grace Swan's Salmon Wellington from Bluenose Lodge, Lunenburg, and Salmon with Leek Straw and Mango and Orange Salsa from the Dunes Café and Gardens, Brackley Beach, PEI. Not long ago fresh Atlantic salmon was only available during the early summer. Fish were caught off the coast as they migrated from their ocean home to spawning grounds in the freshwater rivers of Atlantic Canada. Salmon consumed at other times of the year was either canned or frozen.

In the 1980s a decline in wild Atlantic salmon stocks prompted reduction and, later, banning of the commercial salmon fishery. Fortunately, it was found that Atlantic salmon respond well to acquaculture and a thriving, cultivated salmon fishery now provides fresh farmed salmon year-round. The quality of the fish is superb and the taste is exquisite.

Atlantic Canada is also known around the world for its smoked salmon — a delicacy that is sometimes prepared in family-run smokehouses. Fortunate travellers may spot these outlets as they drive throughout the region; we suggest you stop to sample and buy their fare.

Patrons of Maritime restaurants expect fresh, high quality fish and we are pleased to note that the chefs of the region include many salmon recipes in their menus. We hope that you enjoy preparing the selection of recipes offered in this book. *Bon appetit!*

BUYING SALMON

Fresh salmon is extremely perishable so it is important to know how to check for freshness. It should have a slightly sweet odor, bright scales and red gills. The eyes should be clear and slightly bulging and the flesh should bounce back when lightly touched.

When buying fillets or steaks look for firm, moist flesh that is bright in colour. Avoid fish that is blemished or dry around the edges. Find a good fishmarket and build a rapport with the fishmonger; he or she will be able to offer excellent advice.

When buying frozen salmon look for solid product with no dry spots or edges. It should be properly wrapped, and have an ice glaze, but no frost or freezer burn.

As fresh salmon deteriorates rapidly it is best to prepare the fish within hours of purchase. If that is not possible then rinse fish in cold water to which you have added a few drops of lemon juice. Pat dry and store in an airtight container in the coldest section of your refrigerator for **no longer than 2 days.**

Store frozen salmon in freezer for no longer than **2 to 3 months.** If fish thaws do not refreeze.

NUTRITIONAL VALUE

Salmon is protein rich, low in calories and contains Omega-3 polyunsaturated fatty acids. Omega-3 acids, commonly found in cold water fish, significantly reduce blood clotting, lowering the risk of heart attack and stroke. A 100-gram (3.5 ounce) serving contains 2.54 g of polyunsaturated fat, 1.28 g of Omega-3 fatty acid, 34.7 mg cholesterol and 143 calories.

PREPARATION

Here are some hints to successfully preparing salmon in order to preserve the texture and prevent overcooking. The Canadian Fisheries rule is to measure fish at its thickest section and cook it for 10 minutes per inch (5 to 7 minutes per cm). Double the cooking time for frozen fish. This rule is reliable and applies to cooking steaks, fillets or whole fish, whether baked, broiled, grilled, poached or fried. For microwave cooking, cook 3–5 minutes per pound of fish in a 700 watt oven, or follow manufacturer's directions.

To test for doneness, insert a knife into the thickest part; the juices should run clear and the flesh should be opaque, moist and flake easily.

APPETIZERS

almon is, oh, so much more than a sandwich ingredient! We found Maritime chefs preparing delectable dishes using this beautiful pink fish. Salmon Bisque from the Normaway Inn and the Pines' rendition of Marinated Salmon are two of our favourites.

◀ *A delicious start to an elegant meal, Smoked Salmon Appetizer Plate from Wolfville's Blomidon Inn.*

SMOKED SALMON APPETIZER PLATE

THE BLOMIDON INN, WOLFVILLE, NS

The ultimate, traditional smoked salmon appetizer (see photo page 6).

mixed lettuces to serve 4–6 (romaine, leaf, bibb, etc.)

12 ounces smoked salmon, thinly sliced

1 red onion, thinly sliced

2 tablespoons capers, drained

4–6 lemon wedges

kale leaves

Cream Cheese Chantilly (see below)

melba toast (see below)

Place a few pieces of lettuce and kale at the top of serving plates. Fan 2 to 3 ounces of smoked salmon on the greens. Place 5 or 6 rings of onion and the capers over the smoked salmon. Drizzle Cream Cheese Chantilly over the salmon and onion. Garnish with pieces of melba toast and lemon wedges. Serves 4–6.

Cream Cheese Chantilly

1/2 cup cream cheese, softened

1/4 cup sour cream

1/4 cup mayonnaise

light cream (10% mf)

Blend together cream cheese, sour cream and mayonnaise. Add enough cream to reach a pouring consistency. Makes 1 cup.

Melba Toast

Cut a baguette on an angle in 1/4-inch slices. Spread with garlic butter and toast in a preheated 350°F oven until lightly golden.

Salmon Salad Niçoise

This is a variation on the traditional Salad Niçoise. Serve it with hot crusty rolls to make a substantial luncheon entrée.

1 garlic clove, halved

1/2 pound cooked fresh green beans

1 can artichoke hearts, drained and quartered

2 tomatoes, cut in wedges

1 pound salmon, cooked and in chunks

1/2 cup pitted black olives, halved

2 tablespoons anchovy fillets, chopped

vinaigrette (recipe follows)

Romaine and leaf lettuce to serve four

3 hard-cooked eggs, in wedges

Rub salad bowl with garlic. Combine beans, artichokes, tomatoes, salmon, olives and anchovies in bowl. Drizzle vinaigrette over ingredients and gently stir to mix. Arrange lettuce on serving plates and top with salad. Garnish with hard-cooked eggs. Serves 4–6.

Vinaigrette

1/4 teaspoon salt

1/4 teaspoon dry mustard

1/4 teaspoon freshly ground black pepper

1 garlic clove, crushed

2 tablespoons lemon juice

1/3 cup extra virgin olive oil

In a food processor combine salt, mustard, pepper, garlic and lemon juice. Process while gradually pouring in olive oil. Refrigerate.

MARINATED SALMON

THE PINES RESORT HOTEL, DIGBY, NS

Seviche or marinated raw fish is very popular as an hors d'oeuvre. The chemical action of fresh lime juice on the delicate salmon "cooks" the seafood.

4 ounces salmon fillet, boned and skinned

1/4 cup fresh lime juice

6 tablespoons extra virgin olive oil

6 drops Tabasco sauce

4 drops Worcestershire sauce

salt and freshly ground pepper, to taste

1 baguette, cut into 12 slices

2 tablespoons fresh herbs, chopped (dill, oregano, basil, etc.)

salad greens for 4 servings

With a sharp knife, cut the salmon in very thin slices and arrange on a shallow non-metallic platter. Cover with plastic wrap and reserve in refrigerator.

Make vinaigrette by whisking together lime juice, olive oil, Tabasco, Worcestershire, salt and pepper. Reserve. Toast the slices of baguette on both sides and reserve.

Add the fresh herbs to the vinaigrette and with a brush spread it evenly onto the salmon slices. Gently turn the salmon and brush other side. Marinate the salmon for 5 minutes, until it is opaque.

Toss remaining vinaigrette with the salad greens and distribute onto 4 plates. Place marinated salmon on toasted baguettes, season with freshly ground pepper and arrange on top of greens. Serve immediately. Serves 4.

The Pines Resort Hotel's rendition of Marinated Salmon. ▶

SCRAMBLED EGGS WITH NOVA SCOTIA SMOKED SALMON

*Whether you serve these eggs as a luncheon entrée or a special breakfast treat,
we are sure your guests will ask for the recipe.*

6 large eggs

2 tablespoons light cream (10% mf)

dash salt and pepper

1 1/2 tablespoons butter

4 ounces smoked salmon cut into thin strips

chopped fresh chives, as garnish

Whisk together eggs, cream, salt and pepper. Melt butter in a skillet over medium heat and add eggs. Stir with a spatula until eggs are almost set, about 5 minutes. Fold in salmon and cook about 1 minute longer. Transfer to serving plates and sprinkle with chives.
Serves 3–4.

THE MARKLAND'S CAPE BRETON FISH CHOWDER

THE MARKLAND COASTAL RESORT, DINGWALL, NS

*Succulent pink salmon, scallops and Atlantic blue mussels in their shells
give this chowder tremendous eye appeal.*

1/4 cup butter

3 potatoes, peeled and diced

2 stalks celery, diced

1 carrot, diced

1 onion, diced

1 clove garlic, minced

1/4 cup flour

6 cups stock, chicken or seafood

1/2 pound skinless salmon fillet, 1-inch cubes

1/4 pound scallops, sliced if large

1 pound mussels, scrubbed and debearded

1/2 cup light cream (10% mf)

1/4 cup heavy cream (35% mf)

4 teaspoons fresh dill, chopped (1 teaspoon dried)

4 teaspoons fresh basil, chopped (1 teaspoon dried)

1/4 teaspoon freshly ground pepper

In a large heavy saucepan, melt butter over medium-high heat; sauté potatoes, celery, carrot, onion and garlic, stirring, for 8 minutes or until softened. Stir in flour and gradually whisk in 5 cups of the stock. Bring to a boil, reduce heat and simmer, covered, for about 10 minutes or until vegetables are tender.

Meanwhile in a separate saucepan, bring remaining stock to a boil. Reduce heat to simmer and poach salmon cubes for 1 minute, remove with slotted spoon and reserve. Poach scallops for 1 minute, remove with slotted spoon and reserve with salmon. Prepare mussels, being careful to remove any that have broken shells or do not close. Add mussels to stock, cover and cook for 4 minutes or until they open. Remove mussels with a slotted spoon, discarding any that do not fully open; reserve with other seafood.

Strain poaching liquid into vegetable mixture; add light cream, heavy cream, dill, basil and pepper and heat through being careful not to boil. Add reserved seafood, heat until steaming and serve immediately. Serves 6.

SALMON LOG

A friend gave us this recipe years ago and it has become a family favourite. Prepare it a day in advance so the log will become firm and the flavours blend. We substituted light cream cheese without compromising the taste.

8 ounces salmon fillet, cooked or 1 7-ounce can of salmon

8 ounces cream cheese, softened

1 tablespoon lemon juice

2 tablespoons grated onion

1 tablespoon horseradish

1/4 teaspoon salt

1/2 cup walnuts, finely chopped

2-3 tablespoons parsley, finely chopped

Flake salmon and combine with cheese, lemon juice, onion, horseradish and salt. Form into a log shape and chill for 30 minutes. Combine walnuts and parsley and roll log in mixture. Serve with assorted crackers.

SALMON BISQUE

THE NORMAWAY INN, MARGAREE VALLEY, NS

David MacDonald of the Normaway Inn shared this delicious bisque recipe with us several years ago. For a low-fat version we tested the recipe using two cups milk instead of the milk-light cream combination.

2 cups water

1/4 cup white wine

1 celery stalk with leaves, sliced

1 bay leaf

5 peppercorns

1 pound salmon

1/4 cup butter

1/4 cup chopped onion

1/4 cup chopped celery (2nd amount)

3 tablespoons flour

1 teaspoon salt

1 cup light cream (10% mf) and 1 cup milk

1 cup tomato juice

2 tablespoons chopped fresh parsley

salt and pepper to taste

In a saucepan combine the water, wine, celery, bay leaf and peppercorns, and bring to a boil. Poach salmon in boiling liquid until barely cooked. Remove and cool slightly, trim skin and bones, flake meat and set aside. Strain and reserve poaching liquid.

Heat butter and sauté onion and celery (2nd amount) over low heat for 5 minutes. Add flour and salt, stir to combine, remove from heat. Combine 1 cup of poaching liquid, cream and milk, and gently whisk into flour mixture. Return to moderate heat and cook, stirring constantly, until smooth and thickened. Add tomato juice, parsley, seasonings and flaked salmon. Return to serving temperature, being careful not to allow bisque to boil. Serves 4.

SALMON PATÉ

HADDON HALL, CHESTER, NS

For a spectacular presentation the chef garnished this paté with fresh dill and leeks, set in an herb sauce.

1 1/2 pounds skinless salmon fillet

4 egg whites

3 tablespoons white wine

generous dash salt and white pepper

1 cup heavy cream (35% mf)

Preheat oven to 350°F. Using the metal blade, process salmon in a food processor until smooth. Transfer salmon to a mixing bowl, add egg whites and beat at top speed for 2 minutes or until well blended. Reduce speed to medium, add wine and seasonings. Add cream and mix for a few more minutes until mixture thickens. Grease, then line with waxed paper a 2-cup paté form. Bake in a water bath for 50–60 minutes. Check carefully the last 10 minutes and do not overcook. Remove from oven and cool in water, then refrigerate. Before serving, unmold and garnish as desired. Serves 12.

Salmon Paté from Haddon Hall, Chester. ▶

PATÉ OF SMOKED SALMON

Seafood patés are easy to make and delicately delicious. Prepare several hours
in advance so that flavours can blend.

1/2 pound smoked Atlantic salmon, diced

1/2 cup unsalted butter, softened

1/2 cup onion, finely diced

1 1/2 teaspoons capers, drained

2 tablespoons heavy cream (35%mf)

2 teaspoons fresh lemon juice

1 teaspoon Dijon mustard

few dashes of Tabasco sauce, or to taste

Combine all ingredients in a food processor and process until smooth, frequently scraping down side of bowl with a spatula. Spread paté into serving dish, cover with plastic wrap and refrigerate. Garnish with additional capers and thinly sliced smoked salmon, if desired. Serve with toast points, assorted crackers or fresh bagels. Yields 2 cups.

CHILLED SALMON SALAD MOLD

For optimum presentation, we suggest you prepare this in a fish-shaped mold. Serve on a platter of salad greens, garnished with ripe olives, tomato wedges and radish roses.

2 envelopes unflavoured gelatin

1/2 cup cold water

1 can condensed tomato soup (10 ounces)

8 ounces cream cheese, softened and cut in chunks

1 cup egg-based mayonnaise

1/2 green pepper, diced

1/2 cup celery, diced

1/2 cup onion, diced

1/4 cup drained pickle relish

8 ounces cooked salmon, flaked (or 7 ounces canned)

Sprinkle gelatin over cold water to soften, set aside 5 minutes. Heat soup in a saucepan over medium heat, add cream cheese and beat with a mixer until smooth. Stir in gelatin and mayonnaise. Refrigerate until partially set. Add remaining ingredients and pour into a 5 1/2-cup salad mold. Chill until firm. Serves 6–8.

MARINATED ATLANTIC SALMON WITH A TRIO OF PEPPERCORNS

HALLIBURTON HOUSE INN, HALIFAX, NS

Chef Maurice Pohl uses the acid in fresh lemon juice to "cook" the salmon in this flavourful appetizer.

1 1/2 teaspoon each of dried green, pink and black peppercorns

1/3 cup fresh lemon juice

2 teaspoons coarse sea salt

1/3 cup olive oil

1 pound fresh salmon, sliced 1/4-inch thick

1 lemon, sliced in wedges

1 tablespoon fresh herbs, minced (parsley, basil, oregano)

Coarsely grind peppercorns in a peppermill or crush with a mortar and pestle; place in a small bowl. Gradually whisk lemon juice, salt and olive oil into peppercorns. Spoon 1/2 of this mixture over the bottom of a non-metallic platter. Spread salmon evenly on marinade and cover with remaining mixture. Cover and refrigerate for 2–3 hours.

Carefully remove salmon from marinade and arrange on serving dish. Garnish with lemon wedges and fresh herbs, serve with toast points, crackers or fresh bread. Serves 4–6.

Marinated Atlantic Salmon served with a Trio of Peppercorns will delight the tastebuds. ▶

SMOKED SALMON PARTY QUICHES

Plan to serve more than one of these tasty morsels to your guests.
We are sure they will be the hit of your party!

12 unbaked individual serving pastry shells

2 tablespoons butter

3 mushrooms, finely chopped

1 green onion, finely chopped

1 egg, beaten

1/3 cup sour cream

4 ounces smoked salmon, shredded

Preheat oven to 375°F. Arrange pastry shells on a baking sheet and reserve. Melt butter in a small skillet over medium high heat and saute mushrooms and onion until tender, about 3 minutes. Remove from heat and cool slightly.

In a small bowl combine egg, sour cream and cooled vegetables. Evenly divide shredded salmon in bottom of pastry shells; top with cream mixture and bake 25 minutes. Serve warm. Yields 12 tarts.

LOX MOUSSE

THE MURRAY MANOR BED AND BREAKFAST, YARMOUTH, NS

Smoked Atlantic salmon is an acclaimed delicacy worldwide. At the Murray Manor it is combined with cream cheese to make a delightful spread for melba rounds and assorted crackers.

3 ounces smoked salmon

8 ounces cream cheese

2 tablespoons minced onion

2 teaspoons lemon juice

pepper, to taste

1/4 cup pitted California-style black olives, sliced

Blend together smoked salmon and cream cheese in a food processor. Add onion, lemon juice and season with pepper. Fold in black olives and place in a small bowl. Refrigerate several hours to blend flavours. Serves 8–10.

MAIN COURSES

We have included in this section a wide variety of salmon entrées. Many are suitable for fat-reduced diets. For example, we suggest the quick and easy Grilled Salmon with Choice of Marinades from Lunenburg's Compass Rose Inn or Highland Salmon from Saint John's Inn on the Cove.

◀ *An English favourite, Kedgeree, as served at Bellhill Tea House, Canning, NS.*

KEDGEREE

BELLHILL TEA HOUSE, CANNING, NS

This dish is an English favourite brought back from India during the days of colonial rule. The original dish known as a "kadgeri" featured rice garnished with onions, lentils and eggs; to this the English added smoked fish and a curry-flavoured sauce.

1 cup brown rice

2 1/2 cups water

1/2 teaspoon salt

2 tablespoons butter

1 small onion, chopped

3/4 teaspoon curry powder (or to taste)

2 tablespoons butter (2nd amount)

2 tablespoons flour

pinch of white pepper

1 1/2 cup chicken broth

3/4 lb smoked salmon, thinly sliced

3 eggs, hard-cooked and cut in chunks

parsley for garnish

Combine rice, water and salt in a saucepan; cover and bring to a boil. Reduce heat and simmer until water is absorbed, approximately 25 minutes.

In a large heavy skillet heat 2 tablespoons butter; sauté onion until soft but not brown. Add curry powder, remaining 2 tablespoons butter, flour and white pepper. Whisk in chicken broth, bring to a simmer and reduce sauce to 1 cup.

Add cooked rice to sauce stirring to combine well. Gently fold smoked salmon and eggs into rice. Garnish with chopped fresh parsley. Serves 4.

HERB BAKED SALMON

This recipe is a wonderful way to prepare a whole salmon. Follow the directions for the barbecue or if the weather is inclement, bake in the oven.

3–4 pound salmon, preferably deboned

4 tablespoons olive oil

4 tablespoons fresh lemon juice

1 teaspoon salt

1/4 teaspoon, freshly ground pepper

1 stalk celery with leaves, chopped

1 small onion, finely chopped

2 tablespoons fresh parsley, chopped

1 1/2 teaspoon fresh thyme, chopped
(1/2 teaspoon dried)

1 tablespoon fresh tarragon, chopped
(1 1/2 teaspoon dried)

1 teaspoon fresh rosemary, chopped
(1/4 teaspoon dried)

lemon wedges and parsley, for garnish

Rinse fish and pat dry. With sharp knife make 4 shallow diagonal slashes through skin on both sides. Combine oil and lemon and brush cavity of fish. Sprinkle cavity with salt and pepper. Combine celery, onion, parsley, thyme, tarragon and rosemary; stuff fish with herb mixture and close with skewers. Brush outside of fish with remaining oil and lemon juice.

Place fish on double thickness of foil, wrap and secure. Heat barbecue coals to medium-hot and place foil-wrapped fish on grill. Cook fish 10–12 minutes for every inch of thickness at the thickest part. Halfway through cooking, turn fish to cook on other side. To test for doneness; make a small slit in the foil and with a sharp knife carefully examine flesh. Fish is cooked when flesh flakes easily and turns opaque.

Alternatively, you may want to bake salmon in the oven. Preheat oven to 400°F. Place fish on well oiled baking sheet, and allow 10 minutes for every inch of thickness of fish. Carefully examine flesh with a sharp knife to test for doneness. Fish is cooked when flesh flakes easily and is opaque.

Garnish whole salmon with lemon wedges and fresh parsley. Serves 6–8.

BARBECUED TERIYAKI SALMON

This recipe is so popular in our household that we shovel the snow off the gas barbecue to prepare it during the winter!

2–3 tablespoons teriyaki sauce

4 teaspoons fresh ginger, peeled and grated

1/4 teaspoon sesame oil

1/2 teaspoon canola or vegetable oil

4 salmon fillets, 6 ounces each

fresh parsley sprigs for garnish

Combine teriyaki sauce, ginger and oils. Brush fillets and let stand 10 minutes. Prepare grill by spraying with a no-stick cooking spray. Place salmon fillets on grill, flesh side down and cook on low to medium heat for approximately 6 to 7 minutes. Flip over to skin side and cook 2 to 3 minutes until fish flakes easily and is opaque. Serves 4.

HIGHLAND SALMON

INN ON THE COVE, SAINT JOHN, NB

Innkeeper Ross Mavis tells us that this marinade will enhance but not mask the wonderful flavour of Atlantic salmon. The recipe has been featured on "Tide's Table," a television show filmed at the inn.

4 salmon fillets, 6–8 ounces each

1/2 cup orange juice

1/3 cup scotch whisky

1 1/2 tablespoons maple syrup

zest of an orange (thinly grated peel)

1 tablespoon grainy Dijon mustard

2 teaspoons Worcestershire sauce

1 teaspoon freshly ground black pepper

3/4 teaspoon salt

Place salmon fillets in a shallow glass baking dish. Combine remaining ingredients in a mixing bowl and pour over salmon. Refrigerate 2–4 hours, turning fish at least once.

1 to 2 hrs wasn't enough

Remove salmon from marinade and broil or barbecue about 4 minutes on each side, turning once until fish flakes easily and is opaque. Baste with marinade during last minute of cooking. Serves 4.

Highland Salmon, more than a hint of its Scottish roots, Inn on the Cove, Saint John, NB. ▶

SALMON IN A CREAMY DILL SAUCE

THE DRURY LANE STEAK HOUSE, AULAC, NB

This is a marvellous combination of flavours. At the Drury Lane they serve it on a bed of spinach fettucini with a slice of lemon and a sprig of fresh dill for garnish.

poaching liquid (recipe follows)

4 salmon steaks, 8 ounces each

1/2 cup butter

4 cups light cream (10% mf)

1/2 cup parmesan cheese

1 1/2 tablespoons fresh dill

dash of nutmeg

salt and pepper, to taste

lemon wedges and fresh dill for garnish

Prepare poaching liquid as described below. Place the salmon steaks in the liquid and gently simmer 12–15 minutes. Remove steaks with a slotted spatula and cool.

Combine butter and light cream in a large saucepan and simmer over low heat until slightly thickened, about 10 minutes. Stir in parmesan, dill, nutmeg, salt and pepper. Break salmon steaks into bite size chunks, being careful to remove bones and skin. Stir gently into sauce and return to serving temperature. Spoon over pasta or rice, garnished with lemon wedges and fresh dill. Serves 4.

Poaching liquid *(provided by authors)*

4 cups water

1 cup dry white wine

1 stalk celery with leaves, chopped finely

1 large carrot, sliced

1 medium onion, sliced

1 bay leaf

8 peppercorns

1/2 teaspoon salt

2 sprigs fresh parsley

Combine water, wine, celery, carrot, onion, bay leaf, peppercorns, salt and parsley in a large skillet and simmer 30 minutes.

Chef Sharon Meldrum serves her Salmon in a Creamy Dill Sauce on a bed of fettucini. ▶

SALMON IN SAOR (MARINATED COLD SALMON)

DA MAURIZIO DINING ROOM, HALIFAX, NS

*This salmon dish is easily prepared in advance and is a delicious entrée
for a warm summer's evening.*

4 salmon fillets, 6 ounces each

1/4 cup flour

3 tablespoon vegetable oil

1 small Spanish onion, finely sliced

1/2 cup sultana raisins

1 cup medium white wine

1 tablespoon sugar

2 tablespoons fresh lemon juice

2 tablespoons balsamic vinegar

salt and pepper to taste

Dredge salmon fillets in flour to coat. Heat 1 tablespoon of the vegetable oil in a skillet over medium high heat and sauté the fillets until the flesh flakes easily and is opaque. Remove and place on a paper towel to absorb excess cooking oil. Arrange salmon in a shallow serving dish and reserve.

Heat remaining 2 tablespoons vegetable oil in a skillet, add onion and sauté until golden. Add raisins, wine and sugar and simmer until the wine is reduced by half. Add lemon juice and balsamic vinegar, season with salt and pepper and simmer for 1 minute.

Pour the hot marinade over the salmon and chill for 2 hours, basting occasionally. Serve chilled, garnished with lemon slices. Serves 4.

MEDITERRANEAN BAKED SALMON

"Light" cooking at its flavourful best — we love serving this easy-to-prepare dish for company. Guests think we have been slaving for hours and we never tell them the truth!

6 salmon steaks, 6 ounces each

1 teaspoon olive oil

1 teaspoon butter

1 1/4 cup dry white wine

1 cup fish stock or bottled clam juice

1 cup coarsely chopped tomatoes (preferably Italian Plum)

12 black olives, pitted and sliced

1 to 2 teaspoons saffron threads

2 large garlic cloves, minced

1/2 teaspoon dried tarragon

1/4 teaspoon dried thyme

1/2 teaspoon crushed bay leaves

salt and pepper to taste

Preheat oven to 400°F. Briefly sauté salmon on each side in oil and butter for approximately one minute, over medium-high heat in a large stovetop casserole or ovenproof skillet. Remove salmon to a platter. Add remaining ingredients to casserole and stir well to combine. Bring sauce to a boil, lower heat and simmer, uncovered for 10 minutes.

Remove casserole from heat, add reserved salmon steaks and place in oven. Bake, uncovered, until salmon is lightly pink and done to taste, approximately 10 minutes.

Arrange salmon on platter and spoon sauce over. Serves 6.

FILLET OF SALMON WITH CREAM LEEK SAUCE

QUACO INN, ST. MARTINS, NB

At the Quaco Inn, fresh Atlantic salmon is almost always on the menu.
The presentation in the photo opposite is a house speciality.

4 salmon fillets, 5 ounces each

3 tablespoons butter

2 green onions, cut in thin 3-inch julienne strips

1 leek, white part only, cut in thin 3-inch julienne strips

2/3 cup fish stock

1 cup heavy cream

1 1/2 tablespoons dry white vermouth

salt and pepper, to taste

pinch of cayenne pepper

fresh dill sprigs, for garnish

Rinse and pat dry salmon fillets, set aside.

Melt butter over medium heat in a skillet. Cut green onions and leeks in very thin strands and sauté in butter until softened, about 4 minutes. Add fish stock and continue to cook until vegetables are tender. Add cream and boil until mixture begins to thicken, about 8 minutes. Add vermouth and simmer gently 5 minutes. Season with salt, pepper and cayenne.

Grill salmon steaks, 3 inches from heat source, for 5 minutes or until salmon flakes easily and is opaque. To serve, nap steaks with sauce and garnish with a sprig of fresh dill. Serves 4.

Grilled Salmon accompanied by new potatoes and summer vegetables, ▶
Quaco Inn, St. Martins, NB.

SALMON ROULADE WITH DILL SAUCE

MARSHLANDS INN, SACKVILLE, NB

This recipe is an excellent choice for an elegant dinner party. Prepare your salmon in advance and refrigerate up to three hours before baking. For best results, we suggest that the dill sauce be made just prior to serving.

4 salmon fillets, boneless and skinless, 4 to 5 ounces each

6 ounces fresh spinach

8 ounces fresh mushrooms

2 tablespoons butter

1 1/2 tablespoons heavy cream (35% mf)

salt and pepper

dill sauce (recipe follows)

Preheat oven to 400°F. Lay fillets on a piece of plastic wrap and cover with a second piece of wrap. Gently pound fillets, one at a time, to a size approximately 8 inches square.

Remove stems from spinach and blanch 20 seconds in boiling salted water. Immediately refresh with ice water and drain. Squeeze out moisture and place on paper towel to dry.

Clean mushrooms and grate with a cheese grater. Melt the butter in a small saucepan over medium heat, add mushrooms and sauté until liquid has evaporated, being careful not to brown. Pour in cream and continue cooking to reduce slightly. Season with salt and pepper and set aside to cool.

To prepare roulade, lay one salmon fillet flat and remove top piece of plastic wrap. Cover salmon with a layer of spinach leaves, then with a thin layer of mushrooms. Gently roll the fillet jellyroll-fashion and place on a piece of aluminum foil that has been brushed with butter and sprinkled with salt and pepper. Repeat procedure until you have four salmon packets. Place in oven and bake. To serve, remove salmon from foil and slice on an angle with a sharp serrated knife. Divide dill sauce between four serving plates and top with salmon slices. Serves 4.

Dill sauce

1/2 cup white wine

1/2 cup heavy cream (35% mf)

1/4 pound butter, cut in cubes

1 1/2 tablespoons fresh dill or 1 1/2 teaspoons dried

salt and pepper, to taste

Place wine in a small saucepan over medium high heat and reduce by one half. Add cream and reduce by one half again. Whisk in butter, a few cubes at a time, add dill and season with salt and pepper. Serve immediately.

The Marshlands Inn's Salmon Roulade and Dill Sauce, Sackville, NB. ▶

BISTRO-STYLE SALMON WITH DIJON MUSTARD SAUCE

Serve this delightful dish hot or cold, depending on the weather. Any leftover sauce will keep, refrigerated, for a week and is great on sandwiches.

6 salmon steaks, 6 ounces each

1 1/2 cups dry white wine

1/4 cup shallots or green onions, minced

Preheat oven to 400°F. Place salmon steaks in a large baking dish and add enough wine to cover. Sprinkle with shallots. Bake, uncovered, basting often with wine until fish is lightly pink and done to taste approximately 12–15 minutes. Serves 6.

Dijon Mustard Sauce

1/3 cup Dijon mustard

1/3 cup plain yogurt

1 1/2 tablespoons liquid honey

3 tablespoons fresh dill, minced (2 teaspoons dried)

1/3 cup fresh lemon juice

Combine all ingredients in a small bowl and whisk until smooth. Serve over salmon. Refrigerate remaining sauce. Makes approximately 1 cup.

HONEY MUSTARD GLAZED SALMON

NEMO'S RESTAURANT, HALIFAX, NS

Brian Trainor of Nemo's Restaurant developed this succulent sauce for his salmon dish. He tells us that the glaze can be used on lamb or ribs and is equally tasty served as a dipping sauce for shrimp and scallops.

2 tablespoons finely chopped onion

2/3 cup whole grain Dijon-style mustard

1/2 cup liquid honey

6 salmon steaks or fillets, 6–8 ounces each

1/4 cup flour

1/4 teaspoon salt

1/8 teaspoon white pepper

1–2 tablespoons vegetable oil

Preheat oven to 325°F. Combine onion, mustard and honey in a saucepan and cook over low heat until blended. Reserve and keep warm.

Lightly dust the salmon with flour, season with salt and pepper. Heat oil over high heat in a heavy oven-proof skillet. Add fillets and sear, turning once. Place skillet in oven and bake 4–5 minutes, until done. Remove skillet from oven. Turn oven to broil. Pour glaze over salmon and broil 30 seconds or until brown and bubbly. Serves 6.

*Sweet and tangy Honey Mustard Glazed Salmon ▶
from Nemo's Restaurant, Halifax, NS.*

GRILLED SALMON WITH A CHOICE OF MARINADES

THE COMPASS ROSE INN , LUNENBURG, NS

Rodger Pike from Lunenburg's Compass Rose Inn shares two excellent marinades. Why not prepare both and keep them on hand to impress friends and family. Rodger tells us that the marinades lend themselves well to any fresh seafood.

6 fresh salmon steaks or fillets, 6 ounces each

marinade of choice

Before igniting barbecue, prepare grill by spraying with a non-stick cooking spray. Heat barbecue, brush salmon with marinade and place on grill. Cook on low to medium heat for 7–10 minutes, brushing with the marinade two additional times. The fish is cooked when it flakes easily and the flesh is opaque.

Store leftover marinade in refrigerator for later use.

Orange sesame marinade

1/4 cup light soya sauce

3 tablespoons red wine vinegar

1 tablespoon honey

1/2 cup fresh orange juice

1/4 cup peanut oil

3 tablespoons sesame oil

1 tablespoon hot chili oil

2 garlic cloves, crushed

1 tablespoon fresh ginger, minced

Combine all marinade ingredients in a small, deep bowl and whisk until emulsified. Refrigerate so flavours will blend.

Herbes de Provence marinade

1/4 cup fresh lemon juice

1/4 cup dry white wine

2 tablespoons red wine vinegar

1/4 cup olive oil

1/4 cup vegetable oil

1/4 teaspoon each: marjoram, thyme, summer savory, powdered bay leaf, basil, oregano, rosemary and sage

2 tablespoons coarsely ground black pepper

sea salt to taste

Combine all marinade ingredients in a small, deep bowl and whisk until emulsified. Refrigerate so flavours will blend.

POACHED ATLANTIC SALMON

SHAW'S HOTEL, BRACKLEY BEACH, PEI

This whole poached salmon is a house speciality at Shaw's. It is easy to prepare and delicious when napped with their White Wine Sauce.

2 1/2 to 3 pound fresh Atlantic salmon

cold water to cover fish

1 cup dry white wine

1/2 cup lemon juice

6-8 peppercorns

1 teaspoon salt

1 large carrot, peeled and diced

1 medium onion, peeled and sliced

1 large stalk celery with top, sliced

1/4 cup fresh tarragon, chopped

2 tablespoons butter

2 tablespoons flour

2/3 cup milk

1/3 cup heavy cream (35% mf)

2 tablespoons dry white wine

salt and white pepper to taste

1 tablespoon parsley, chopped

Rinse and pat dry salmon. Place on a rack in a poaching pan and cover with water. Add wine, lemon juice, peppercorns, salt, carrot, onion, celery and tarragon and bring to a boil. Reduce heat and simmer, covered, 2 minutes per pound. Turn off heat and let stand in water one hour. Drain, remove skin and place on a serving platter.

To prepare sauce, melt butter and stir in flour to form a roux. Cook until bubbly, 1–2 minutes, stirring constantly. Whisk in milk, cream, and wine. Cook over medium heat until thickened. Adjust seasonings and serve over salmon. Serves 4–6.

SALMON WITH LEEK STRAW AND MANGO AND ORANGE SALSA

THE DUNES CAFÉ AND GARDENS, BRACKLEY BEACH, PEI

Scott Carr, chef at the Dunes Café and Gardens grows fresh flowers and herbs for use in the restaurant. Not only is his salmon dish delicious, but artistically presented on local pottery.

2 leeks

1 tablespoon cornstarch

3–4 tablespoons vegetable oil

1 mango, peeled and diced

1 orange, peeled and diced

1 sweet red pepper, diced

1 red onion, diced

2 tablespoons cilantro, chopped

1 tablespoon balsamic vinegar

salt and pepper, to taste

4 salmon fillets, 6 ounces each

Prepare leek straw by removing the tough green part of the stocks. The sweet onion flavour you wish to capture in this recipe is found in the white part of the leek. Peel off any dry outer leaves and rinse thoroughly, then pat dry. Slice into fine 3-inch long julienne strips, then dust with cornstarch. Heat oil over medium high heat in a small skillet, immerse leeks until golden brown. Remove from oil with a slotted spatula and place on paper towel to drain.

Prepare mango, orange, red pepper and onion and combine in a bowl. Stir in cilantro, vinegar, salt and pepper. Set salsa aside to allow flavours to blend.

Preheat oven to 325°F. Sear salmon on a hot grill, turning once. Remove to oven and bake 6–7 minutes until done. Serve on a bed of leek straw, topped with a spoonful of mango and orange salsa.

Salmon with Leek Straw and a Mango and Orange Salsa dramatically ▶ presented by Chef Scott Carr at the Dunes Café and Gardens.

SALMON WELLINGTON

THE BLUENOSE LODGE, LUNENBURG, NS

Grace Swan also offers a "heart smart" version of this recipe by substituting milk for cream and margarine for butter in the white sauce; however, she feels that you must use butter in the Hollandaise Sauce.

1 to 1 1/4 pounds piece of salmon

1/2 cup dry white wine

1 tablespoon lemon juice

1/2 teaspoon each salt and white pepper

1 bay leaf

water

2 tablespoons butter or margarine

2 tablespoons flour

1/4 teaspoon freshly ground black pepper

pinch of salt (2nd amount)

1/3 cup reserved poaching liquid

2/3 cup cream or milk

frozen puff pastry

1 egg white mixed with 1 teaspoon water

Rinse and pat dry salmon. Place in a deep skillet and combine white wine, lemon juice, salt, pepper and bay leaf with enough water to cover fish. Bring to a gentle boil and simmer, covered, until fish is cooked, allowing approximately 10 minutes per inch of thickness. Drain, reserving liquid. Skin, debone and flake salmon.

Melt butter in a small saucepan. Whisk in flour and cook over medium heat for one minute stirring constantly. Add black pepper and salt.

Gradually stir in 1/3 cup poaching liquid and cream or milk. Stir constantly until sauce comes to a boil and thickens. Taste and adjust seasonings if necessary. Gently blend sauce and flaked fish.

Preheat oven to 400°F. Roll out puff pastry to four 6-inch squares. Prepare eggwash by whisking together egg white and water. Divide salmon mixture between puff pastry squares and fold pastry over salmon envelope-style. Seal edges with eggwash. Place packets on a greased cookie sheet, seam side down. Brush tops with eggwash and score so steam can escape. Bake about 20 minutes until golden. Serve on a bed of Hollandaise Sauce. Serves 4.

Easy Hollandaise Sauce with Dill

The Chef at the Bluenose Lodge tells us that dill freezes very well so it is easy to have on hand. Just snip off what you need with scissors and return to freezer!

3 egg yolks

2 tablespoons lemon juice

3 tablespoons fresh dill or 2 teaspoons dried

1/2 cup very hot melted butter

In a food processor, blend egg yolks, lemon juice and dill for 10 seconds. Continue to process and slowly add melted butter in a steady stream. Serve immediately.

Baked Salmon Wellington from Bluenose Lodge, Lunenburg, NS, ▶ can be accompanied by the perennial favourite, Hollandaise Sauce.

SALMONE AL CAPPUCCIO
(SALMON WRAPPED IN CABBAGE WITH SEAFOOD SAUCE)

LA PERLA RESTAURANT, DARTMOUTH, NS

Pearl MacDougal of La Perla Restaurant takes great care with food presentation and these colourful bundles of seafood are an example of her artistry.

8 large leaves of cabbage, preferably red

4 salmon fillets, 4 to 5 ounces each

4 to 5 tablespoons clarified butter

3 tablespoons garlic butter

4 ounces shrimp, peeled, deveined and roughly chopped

4 ounces scallops, roughly chopped

4 ounces fresh lobster, roughly chopped

1/3 cup dry sherry

1 1/2 cups heavy cream (35% mf)

salt and pepper to taste

dash paprika

Preheat oven to 300°F. Blanch cabbage leaves in boiling salted water until tender and pliable. Cool in ice water. Pat dry, then wrap around salmon.

Melt butter over medium high heat in a large skillet and sauté cabbage-salmon envelopes, about 2 minutes per side, turning once. Place envelopes in oven and bake until salmon is cooked, 7–10 minutes depending upon thickness.

To prepare sauce, melt garlic butter in a medium skillet over high heat; add seafood and sauté 2 minutes. Deglaze pan with sherry. Pour in cream and boil to reduce to a rich creamy sauce. Season with salt and pepper. To serve, cover plate with sauce, top with salmon and sprinkle with paprika. Serves 4.

Salmon Wrapped in Cabbage with a seafood sauce as served at LaPerla Restaurant, ▶ Dartmouth, NS.

BLACKENED SALMON WITH BUTTER SAUCE

THE INN ON THE LAKE, WAVERLEY, NS

At the Inn on the Lake this dish is served with fresh steamed vegetables, garnished with lemon and lime slices, sprigs of parsley and butter sauce.

6 salmon fillets or steaks, 6 ounces each

2 tablespoons Cajun spices

2 tablespoons vegetable oil

lemon and lime slices, for garnish

fresh parsley, for garnish

3 tablespoons white wine

1/4 teaspoon black peppercorns

1/4 teaspoon rosemary

3 tablespoons heavy cream (35% mf)

1/2 lb. unsalted butter

Roll salmon in Cajun spices until well covered. Heat oil in a heavy bottomed frying pan until very hot. Add salmon, serving side down and sear fish, turning once. Place salmon in oven to finish cooking, approximately 5–10 minutes.

Place wine, peppercorns and rosemary in a small saucepan over medium heat, reduce by half. Add cream and reduce until thickened. Cut butter into cubes and add to cream, a few pieces at a time, whisking to blend. Strain and serve with salmon steaks, garnished with lemon and lime slices and parsley. Serves 6.

Spice up salmon with cajun-style Blackened Salmon from the dining room ▶ of the Inn on the Lake, Waverley, NS.

SALMON AND SPINACH LASAGNE

DUFFERIN INN AND SAN MARTELLO DINING ROOM, SAINT JOHN, NB

*Axel Begner of the Dufferin Inn serves this salmon lasagne with
a Caesar salad and warm garlic bread.*

8 ounces lasagne sheets

1 1/4 pounds boneless and skinless salmon fillets

16 ounces fresh spinach, stems removed and rinsed

2 cups Bechamel Sauce (recipe follows)

salt and pepper to taste

1/4 cup freshly grated Parmesan cheese

4 ounces grated mozzarella cheese

chopped fresh parsley or chives for garnish

Prepare lasagne sheets following manufacturer's directions, drain and set aside. Check salmon for bones and cut in 1/2-inch slices. Blanch the prepared spinach in boiling salted water for 1 minute, drain and press firmly to remove water. Prepare Bechamel Sauce and set aside.

Preheat oven to 350°F. Spread a small amount of sauce in a greased 8" x 10" baking pan. Add a layer of lasagne sheets. Continue with a layer of salmon, then spinach and sauce, one layer at a time. Cover the last layer with

sauce, sprinkle with Parmesan and mozzarella and bake for 40–50 minutes. Sprinkle with chopped parsley or chives. Serves 4.

Bechamel Sauce *(supplied by authors)*

2 tablespoons butter

2 tablespoons flour

2 cups milk

1/2 teaspoon salt

1/4 teaspoon white pepper

pinch of ground nutmeg (optional)

2 egg yolks

In a large saucepan melt butter over medium heat; whisk in flour; cook, without browning, about 3 minutes. Gradually whisk in milk and bring to a boil, stirring constantly. Stir in salt, pepper and nutmeg. In a small bowl beat egg yolks lightly and stir in a little of the hot mixture. Blend thoroughly, then stir back into the saucepan. Continue to cook sauce, stirring constantly until thickened. Remove from heat and reserve.

Salmon and Spinach Lasagne served at the Dufferin Inn, Saint John, NB. ▶

CUMIN-CRUSTED SALMON
WITH ROAST CORN POLENTA AND BASIL PEA BROTH

THE INN AT BAY FORTUNE, BAY FORTUNE, PEI

Chef Michael Smith always applies his culinary expertise and creativity in an innovative manner. His treatment of this complete, three-recipe entrée is no exception; the flavours are tantalizingly subtle and the presentation (see photo opposite) is impressive.

Cumin-Crusted Salmon

1 cup cornmeal

1 teaspoon paprika

1 tablespoon ground cumin

2 teaspoons salt

1 teaspoon freshly ground, black pepper

2 tablespoons butter

6 salmon steaks, 6 ounces each

Preheat oven to 400°F. Combine cornmeal, paprika, cumin, salt and pepper in a shallow dish. Dredge salmon in cornmeal mixture to coat evenly. Heat a heavy ovenproof skillet over high heat; add butter and salmon steaks. Brown on one side (approximately 1 minute), turn steaks and finish cooking in oven for 8–10 minutes, until fish flakes easily and is opaque. To serve; drizzle Basil Pea Broth over salmon steaks and accompany with Roast Corn Polenta. Serves 6.

Basil Pea Broth

1 1/2 cups celery or carrot juice

2 teaspoons cornstarch

1 cup peas

salt and pepper to taste

1/2 cup fresh basil, chopped

Process chopped celery stalks in a food processor until puréed. Press purée through a fine sieve to extract juice. Measure 1 1/2 cups celery juice.

Dilute cornstarch in a small amount of water and whisk into celery juice. Heat juice in a small saucepan, cook and stir until sauce is lightly thickened. Add peas, season with salt and pepper and simmer until peas are tender. Stir in basil and serve immediately.

Roast Corn Polenta

1/2 cup butter

1 large onion, diced

4 cups corn kernels

4 cups milk

1 cup fresh parsley, chopped

salt and pepper to taste

2 cups cornmeal

In a heavy-bottomed saucepan, melt butter and sweat onion until golden. Add corn; cook until tender. Add milk, parsley, salt and pepper and bring to a simmer. Whisking vigorously, add cornmeal in a steady stream until fully incorporated. Change to a wooden spoon and continue stirring until polenta pulls away from the sides of the pan, approximately 10 minutes. Roll polenta, between two sheets of plastic wrap, to 1/2" thickness and cut into shapes of choice.

Cumin-crusted Salmon is an original creation of Chef Michael Smith of the Inn at Bay Fortune. ▶

GRILLED SALMON WITH RED BEET COULIS

SCANWAY RESTAURANT, HALIFAX, NS

Fresh Atlantic salmon is a most versitile fish and this dish, served with flavourful red coulis on the side, is sure to be a winner.

3/4 cup beets, cooked and peeled

1/4 cup sugar

1 small orange, peeled and seeded

1/2 cup red wine vinegar

2 tablespoons balsamic vinegar

3 tablespoons butter

4 salmon fillets, 5–6 ounces each

Prepare beets, slice in halves and reserve. In a small skillet over medium heat, heat sugar, stirring constantly. When sugar just begins to melt, add orange pieces and vinegars. Place in a food processor, add butter and puree. Add beets and pulse 2 seconds to blend. Set aside.

Preheat oven to 325°F. Sear salmon on a hot grill, turning once. Remove to oven and bake 6–7 minutes until done. Serve with prepared Red Beet Coulis.

Grilled Salmon with tangy Red Beet Coulis served at Scanway Restaurant, Halifax, NS. ▶

SALMON LOAF

TEA AND TEMPTATIONS ENGLISH TEA ROOM, DARTMOUTH, NS

Cathy Graves of Tea and Temptations serves this delicious salmon loaf with egg or parsley sauce and a green salad on the side.

2 cups cooked fresh salmon or canned, flaked

2 tablespoons lemon juice

3/4 teaspoon salt

2 teaspoons chopped green onions

2 cups soft breadcrumbs

2 eggs, beaten

1/2 cup mayonnaise

1/4 cup milk

Preheat oven to 350°F. Gently combine all ingredients and pour into a greased loaf or bundt pan. Bake for 45 minutes. Serve slices of salmon loaf napped with Egg Sauce.

Egg sauce (supplied by authors)

1 1/2 tablespoons butter

1 1/2 tablespoons flour

1 cup milk, scalded

salt and white pepper, to taste

1 egg, hardboiled and finely diced

1/2 tablespoon capers, drained

Melt butter and whisk in flour, cooking roux for 2 minutes while stirring constantly. Whisk in milk, salt and pepper and bring to a boil. Reduce heat and cook until sauce has thickened. Fold egg and capers into sauce and serve. Yields 1 cup.

Traditional Baked Salmon Log elegantly presented at Tea and Temptations ▶ English Tea Room, Dartmouth, NS.

PAN-FRIED ATLANTIC SALMON ON PRINCE EDWARD ISLAND POTATO AND GARLIC MASH

DALVAY-BY-THE-SEA, DALVAY, PEI

Chef Richard Kemp prides himself in using fresh Island produce and ingredients. This recipe is a classic example of his expertise. He suggests using extra virgin olive oil and cautions that prosciutto is quite salty, hence you should take care when seasoning the salmon or mash!

6 large baking potatoes

salt and pepper, to taste

3 cloves garlic, finely chopped

1/2 cup light cream (10% mf)

1/4 pound butter

8 small ripe tomatoes

3 tablespoons olive oil

1 tablespon fresh basil, chopped

1 tablespoon fresh oregano, chopped

12 thin slices prosciutto

4 salmon fillets, 5 to 6 ounces each

1/4 cup olive oil

2 tablespoons olive oil (2nd amount)

chopped chives, for garnish

Peel potatoes and cut into uniform pieces. Place in a saucepan and cover with water; add a pinch of salt, pepper and two of the garlic cloves. Bring to a boil then simmer until potatoes are cooked through. Drain and mash. Heat light cream and butter and whip into potatoes. Set aside and keep warm.

Preheat oven to 400°F. Plunge tomatoes into boiling water for 20 seconds to blanch, then directly into a bowl of ice water. After tomatoes have cooled, peel and toss in olive oil, remaining garlic, basil and oregano. Place tomatoes in oven for 10 minutes.

Bake prosciutto on a tray in oven until crispy, about 7 minutes. Set aside.

Heat second amount of olive oil until lightly smoking in a skillet. Add salmon fillets and cook for 2 minutes per side. Remove to an ovenproof dish and bake for 5–7 minutes until cooked.

To serve, place potato mash on a large platter, top with salmon fillets and arrange tomatoes around the plate. Garnish with a sprinkling of olive oil, chopped chives and the prosciutto. Serves 4.

Pan-fried Atlantic Salmon is a winner with PEI potatoes and prosciutto, ▶
Dalvay-by-the-Sea, Dalvay, PEI.

POACHED SALMON STEAKS WITH DILL SAUCE

An innkeeper from Prince Edward Island showed us this recipe several years ago.
Unlike the butter-laden Hollandaise, this creamy Dill Sauce offers a
piquant flavour incorporating a small amount of light cream.

4 cups water

1 cup dry vermouth

1 stalk celery with leaves, finely chopped

1 large carrot, sliced

1 medium onion, sliced

1 bay leaf

8 peppercorns

1/2 teaspoon salt

2 sprigs fresh parsley

4 salmon steaks, 6–8 ounces each

2 tablespoons butter

2 tablespoons flour

6 ounces chicken broth

1/4 cup light cream (10% mf)

1 tablespoon fresh dill, chopped (1/2 teaspoon dried)

1 teaspoon sugar

1 tablespoon white vinegar

1 egg yolk from a small egg, beaten

Combine water, vermouth, celery, carrot, onion, bay leaf, peppercorns, salt and parsley in a large skillet and simmer 30 minutes. Place the salmon steaks in the liquid and gently simmer 12–15 minutes. Remove with a slotted spatula to serving plates and drizzle with warm Dill Sauce.

To prepare sauce, melt butter in a saucepan and stir in flour. Gradually mix in chicken broth and light cream. Continue to cook over medium heat, stirring constantly until sauce thickens and bubbles. Add the dill, sugar and vinegar. In a separate bowl beat the egg yolk, stir a small amount of the hot mixture into the yolk, then whisk the egg mixture into the sauce. When reheating, do not allow the sauce to boil. Yields 1 cup sauce.

Serves 4.

QUENELLES OF FRESH ATLANTIC SALMON WITH LEMON AND CHIVE CREAM

ACTON'S GRILL AND CAFÉ, WOLFVILLE, NS

Nicholas Pearce of Acton's suggests that you prepare this delicate dish just before serving time. He accompanies the quenelles with rice pilaf and seasonal greens.

8 ounces fresh salmon, boned and skinned, cut into small pieces

2 egg whites

3/4 cup heavy cream (35% mf)

1 tablespoon fresh dill weed, finely chopped

1 tablespoon fresh lemon juice

1 pinch cayenne pepper

salt and freshly ground white pepper to taste

poaching liquid (see below)

Place salmon pieces and egg whites in the bowl of a food processor. Process with the metal blade into a purée, about 1 minute. Add cream and process for another 20–30 seconds. Remove mixture to a bowl and gently fold in the dill, lemon juice and cayenne pepper. Season with salt and pepper. Chill mixture in the refrigerator for at least 30 minutes.

Poaching liquid

1 small carrot, peeled and diced

2 stalks celery, diced

1 medium onion, diced

1 large bay leaf

1 teaspoon white peppercorns

4 whole cloves

2 cups dry white wine

6 cups water

salt to taste

Combine all ingredients except the salt in a saucepan and bring to a boil. Reduce heat and simmer for 30 minutes. Strain liquid into another saucepan, season with salt and set onto burner to simmer again.

Remove quenelle mixture from refrigerator. With a teaspoon form quenelles to the size of a small walnut and drop into the simmering liquid. Poach 8 minutes, making sure that the poaching liquid does not boil. Remove quenelles with a slotted spoon onto a serving dish and nap with Lemon and Chive Cream. To serve, garnish with a few sprigs of chives and chive blossoms. Serve remaining sauce separately.

QUENELLES CONT'D

Lemon and Chive Cream

1 tablespoon unsalted butter

1 shallot, peeled and finely diced

1 cup dry white wine

Juice of 1 lemon

2 cups heavy cream (35% mf)

1/4 cup fresh chives, finely chopped

salt and freshly ground white pepper to taste

Melt butter in a saucepan, add shallot and cook until translucent. Add wine and lemon juice, bring to a boil and reduce to half volume. Add cream and reduce further until sauce thickens lightly. Remove from heat and add chives. Season with salt and pepper. Keep sauce warm. Serves 6–8 as an appetizer or 4 as a main dish.

From Acton's Grill and Café, Wolfville, NS, Quenelles of Fresh Salmon ▶ are a gourmet's delight.